123

Written and illustrated by Mik Brown

Educational adviser : Jane Salt

Kingfisher Books, Grisewood & Dempsey Ltd., Elsley House, 24–30 Great Titchfield Street, London W1P 7AD. First published in hardcover in 1982 by Kingfisher Books Limited. This revised edition published in 1988.
Copyright © Grisewood & Dempsey Ltd 1982, 1988. All rights reserved.
BRITISH LIBRARY CATALOGUING-IN-PUBLICATION DATA
Brown, Mik. Mik Brown's 123. – 2nd ed. – (Picture Kingfishers).
1. Numeration   I. Title   II. Brown, Mik. Animal fun 123
513'.2 QA141.3   ISBN: 0 86272 265 9
Phototypeset by Southern Positives and Negatives (SPAN), Lingfield, Surrey
Colour separations by Newsele Litho, Milan. Printed in Spain.

Kingfisher Books

1

one mouse in the rain

2

two elephants telephoning

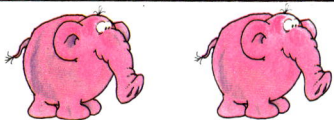

2

3

three crocodiles in canoes

3

4

four bears on cycles

4

5

five tigers playing tunes

5

six tortoises skipping

6

6

seven birds in aeroplanes

7

8

eight cows in bumper cars

8

nine puppies playing ball

9

9

10

ten monkeys swinging

10

Counting Games

What are the elephants doing? One elephant is standing. One elephant is sitting down.

Count how many elephants there are altogether.
1, **2**.

Which hippo is watching his friends boxing?

How many hippos are boxing? 1, **2**.

Count how many hippos there are altogether.
1, 2, **3**.

One lion has no ice-cream. Poor lion!
Can you find him?

How many lions are eating ice-cream?
1, 2, **3**.

Count how many lions there are altogether.
1, 2, 3, **4**.

Which giraffe is not wearing a bow?

How many giraffes are wearing bows?
1, 2, 3, **4**.

Count how many giraffes there are altogether.
1, 2, 3, 4, **5**.

One frog is sitting still. Where is he?

How many frogs are hopping?
1, 2, 3, 4, **5**

Count how many frogs there are altogether.
1, 2, 3, 4, 5, **6**.

One leopard has lost his spots! Can you find him?

How many leopards have spots?
1, 2, 3, 4, 5, **6**.

Count how many leopards there are altogether.
1, 2, 3, 4, 5, 6, **7**.

Most of the snails are wearing sunglasses.
Don't they look funny. Can you find the one
without sunglasses?

Count the snails with sunglasses.
1, 2, 3, 4, 5, 6, **7**.

Count how many snails there are altogether.
1, 2, 3, 4, 5, 6, 7, **8**.

Find the pig with the straight tail.

How many pigs have curly tails?
1, 2, 3, 4, 5, 6, 7, **8**.

Count how many pigs there are altogether.
1, 2, 3, 4, 5, 6, 7, 8, **9**.

One bee has lost his hat. Can you find him?

How many bees are wearing hats?
1, 2, 3, 4, 5, 6, 7, 8, **9**.

Count how many bees there are altogether.
1, 2, 3, 4, 5, 6, 7, 8, 9, **10**.

Can you find?

1 kangaroo

2 mice

3 rabbits

4 elephants

5 zebras

6 lions

Can you find?

7 snakes

8 giraffes

9 birds

10 monkeys

1

2

3

4

5

6

7

8

9

10